HOW TO MAKE LOSS IN BUSINESS

TO ENVISAGE A HUGE PROFIT

GYAN CHAND PATTANAYAK

Made with ♥ on the Notion Press Platform
www.notionpress.com

EYE WANT TO DEDICATE THIS BOOK " HOW TO MAKE LOSS IN BUSINESS " TO ALL THE BUSINESS COMMUNITY ,YOUNG ENTREPRENEURS , BOOK LOVERS , ACADEMIC READERS AND THE FOLLOWERS OF BUSINESS BOOKS.

Contents

Foreword

A COMPLETE FOOT PRINT BASED FOR ENTREPRENEURAL GUIDE FROM BOTTOM TO TOP FOR AN INVISIBLE PROFIT $ LOSS FIGURATION .

world is beautiful when published own book with mother

Preface

WE ALL KNOW BUSINESS HAS ALSO MANY FACES LIKE THE HUMAN HAS AND THE BEST PRACTICE TO UNDERSTAND A BUSINESS, THEN FIRST WE HAVE TO FIGURED OUT THE DIFFERENT TYPES OF FACES OF A HUMAN IN THEIR RESPECTIVE JOURNEY .

Acknowledgements

AN AN AUTHOR , I FIRMLY BELIEVE THAT MARKET HAS A DIFFERENT KIND OF SENTIMENTS LIKE HUMAN HAS AND AS MATTER OF FACT MARKET GOES DOWN WHEN ITS SENTIMENT HURTS AND ALSO GOES UP WHEN IT NOT HURT.

LIKE HUMAN, BUSINESS MARKET HAS ALSO EMOTION WHEN IT MOTION TO DIFEERENT LEVELS.

Prologue

THE ENTREPRENEUR JOURNEY IS NOT THAT SO AS EASY AS ONE CAN IMAGINE BECAUSE WE LIVE IN AN EMOTIONALLY EXPLOITED BUSINESS MARKET . EYE DON'T KNOW WHO INVENTED THIS BUSINESS MODULE AND ITS PLACE OF "ORIGINATION " BUT EYE KNOW ONE THING FORSURE THE RUDIMENT OF ANY BUSINESS IS TO CREATE LOVE FOR A PRODUCT AND SERVES WITH LOVE ..

CHAPTER ONE

HOW TO MAKE LOSS IN BUSINESS

NOW WE HAVE A ONE ONLY HUGE BUSINESS WORLD MARKET WHO DEALT WITH NUMBER OF ESSENTIAL AS WELL AS NON -ESSENTIAL PRODUCTS . WE ARE NOT TALKING ABOUT WHO IS ESSENTIAL PRODUCTS AND WHO IS MAKING NON-ESSENTIAL PRODUCTS BUT THE BOTTOM LINE IS THAT ALL PRODUCTS HAS BEEN MANUFACTURED TO SERVE MANKIND AND THE PRICE WHICH LOCATED ON PRODUCTS IS FOR SURVIVAL . IF THE PRODUCT SURVIVE IN AN EXPLOITED MARKET THEN IT IN-DIRECTLY ALSO HELP THE MANUFACTURER TO SURVIVE IN TERMS OF A LONGER VERSION .

AS AN AUTHOR WHEN EYE FIGURED OUT THIS WORLD MARKET WHICH HAS DIVIDED INTO MANY SEGMENTS BUT BEFORE THIS SEGMENTATION FIRST EYE HAVE TO MADE A CLEAR PICTURE OF THE MARKET FOR SELF CONSIDERATION . EYE ASLO BIT CONFUSED WHEN TRIED TO UNDERSTAND THE MARKET BECAUSE THE MARKET HAS LITERATE USERS AND ILLITERATE USERS AND THE PRODUCT EYE HAVE BEEN TRYING TO DEVELOP FOR THE LITERATE MARKET. EYE DON'T KNOW WHTHER ITS A GLOBAL ISSUE OR NOT BUT ONE THING FORSURE WE CAN'T SELL ROSES IN A POLLUTED MARKET . THIS HUGE WORLD MARKET HAS SOME NATURAL ESSENTIAL PRODUCTS WHICH HAS BEEN DEVELOPED BY NATURE AND ASLO NUMBERS OF PRODUCTS WHICH HAS BEEN DEVELOPED BY HUMAN NATURE AND ULTIMATELY BOTH WORKS FOR HUMAN LITERATION .

FIRST WE HAVE TO UNDERSTAND THAT WHY OUR NATURE DEVELOP PRODUCTS AND ALSO WHY HUMAN NATURE DEVELOP PRODUCTS . WHAT IS THE REAL REASON BEHIND THIS DEVELOPMENT OF ESSENTIAL PRODUCTS AND WHEN FIGURED OUT THE ANSWER ,IT HAS A VERY CLEAR AND RIGHT ANSWER IN SHAPE OF MESSAGE THAT ONLY TO EDUCATE AND LITERATE USERS OF THE MARKET.

ONE OF THE FINEST EXAMPLE OF NATURAL PRODUCTS AN ISLAND

ALL TYPE OF VEGETABLE AND FRUITS AN EXAMPLE OF NATURAL PRODUCTS

HUMAN CREATED PRODUCTS

HUMAN CREATED PRODUCTS WITH NATURE

THESE ARE FEW EXAMPLES OF ESSENTIAL PRODUCTS OFTEN USED BY THE USERS IN DAY TO DAY LIFE AND WHAT WE HAVE LEARNED FROM THIS PRODUCTS THAT THE OTHER NAME OF LIFE IS SURVIVAL OF FITTEST.

LETS BEGIN WITH A FACT THAT WE ARE ALL ENTREPRENEURS WHO BELIEVES TO EDEUCATE AND REEDUCATE USERS THROUGH OUR VISION AS WELL AS OUR PRODUCTS ,WHAT WE MADE TO SERVE.

HOW TO MAKE LOSS IN BUSINESS

EARTH IS A BEAUTIFUL PLATFORM TO SHOWCASE PRODUCTS . WHEN WE MADE A PRODUCT AND MOVE FOR ITS PROMOTION ,IT MUST BE A WELL NARRATIVE ONE BECAUSE OUR PRIME FOCUS IS TO LITERATE THE USERS AND IF WE CREATE ONE LITERATE USER THROUGH OUR PRODUCTS THEN NO NEED TO THINK OF A HUGE NUMBER OF USERS BECAUSE ONE LITERATE USER IS FAR BETTER THAN THOUSANDS OF ILLITERATE USERS . HERE ONE MUST HAVE SOUND KNOWLEDGE OF THEIR ON PRODUCTS BEFORE PITCHING TO OTHERS. AN ENTREPRENEURAL JOURNEY IS NOT SO AN EASY ONE BECAUSE THE JOURNEY OF ENTREPRENEUR IS TO GENERATE LITERATE USER , TO GENERATE EMPLOYMENT , TO GENERATE REVENUE , TO GENERATE SELF PORTFOLIO , TO GENERATE A HEALTHY WORKING ENVIRONMENT ,TO GENERATE WELL NARATIVE PRODUCTS FOR USERS IN AN EXPLOITED MARKET . AS AN AUTHOR OF THIS BOOK "HOW TO MAKE LOSS IN BUSINESS" WHY I OFTEN USE THIS WORD "AN EXPLOITED MARKET" BECAUSE THIS CURRENT MARKET HAS A MIX CULTURAL PRODUCTS . HERE AN ENTREPRENEUR NEED TO CREATE ROBOST FOUNDATION BY SELLING THE INTEREST OF A PATIENCE . THE MORE ONE HAS PATIENCE THE MORE ONE GET INTEREST BECAUSE THE WHOLE CONCEPT OF PATIENCE BELONG TO TIME AND WHEN THE RIGHT TIME COME THEN IT YIELD INTEREST NOT DIVIDEND .

IMAGES FOR HEALTHY UNDERSTANDING (WORK FOR A LITERATE MARKET)

HERE THE QUESTION ARISE THAT, HOW CAN ONE LITERATE THE EXPLOITED MARKET ? AS WE ALL KNOW THAT WE LIVE IN FEDERAL STRUCTURE GOVERNMENT REGION WHERE RIGHT TO EDUCATION IS ONE KIND OF FUNDAMENTAL RIGHTS OF ALL CITIZEN BUT HERE AGAIN THE QUESTION IS WHY WE STILL HAVE AN ILLITERATE MARKET ? EITHER WE DON'T UNDERSTAND BOOKS OR SUBJECTS ARE NOT RELATED TO THE MARKET OR NEED TO INTRODUCE NEW SUBJECTS WHICH WOULD HAVE EASY TO UNDERSTAND AND EASY TO PROMOTE ONE BREATHING LIFE TO EXPLORE IN AN EXPLOITED MARKET . THERE IS A HUGE DIFFERENCE BETWEEN LITERATE MARKET AND ILLITERATE MARKET AND WHEN WE TALK ABOUT LITERATE MARKETS MEANS THESE FELLOW USERS MUST HAVE SOUND KNOWLEDGE ON THEIR RESPECTIVE CONSTITUTION WHICH HAS BEEN WRITTEN BY THEIR INDEPENDENT ANCESTORS AND IT AMENDS TIME TO TIME IN AN ELECTRORAL PROCESS . AS AS AUTHOR I BELIEVE ,IF I DON'T KNOW MY RIGHTS AND MY RESPONSIBILITY THEN I AM NOT A CITIZEN OF THE SAID INDEPENDENT NATION. EVERY INDEPENDENT NATION HAS THEIR OWN CONSTITUTION WHERE ONE FELLOW CITIZEN CAN FIGURE OUT HIS/HER RIGHTS AND HIS/HER RESPONSIBILTY.

IMAGES FOR HEALTHY UNDERSATNDING (ONE MUST LIVE ACCORDING TO CONSTITUTION WHICH HAS WRITTEN FOR FELLOW CITIZENS)

AS AN AUTHOR OF THIS BOOK " HOW TO MAKE LOSS IN BUSINESS" , FIRST JOB FOR ALL GOVERNMENT TO CREATE DISCIPLINE AMONG CITIZENS AND WHEN NATIONS HAVE DISCIPLINE CITIZENS THEN IT AUTOMATICALLY CONVERT INTO A DISCIPLINE MARKET . FOR A DISCIPLINE MARKET FIRST WE HAVE TO CREATE A HEALTHY CONSTITUTION TO RUN A NATION . WHEN WE THINK TO CONSTITUTE A CONSTITUTION THEN IT SHOULD BE CONFINED WITH SHORTER FORMAT OF WITHIN 15 TO 20 ARTICLES WHERE A CITIZEN CAN FIGURED OUT EVERYTHING FROM THEIR RIGHTS TO THEIR DUTIES ,RESPONSIBILTIES FOR NATION .MINIMUM CONSTITUTIONAL ARTICLES MAY CREATE AWARENESS AMONG ALL CITIZENS ,TO UNDERSTAND THEIR RIGHTS IN THIS NATION AND THEIR DUTIES ,RESPONSIBILTIES TO BUILD NATION . AS A AUTHOR I BELIVE IN HEALTHY CONSTITUTION BECAUSE IT ALSO HELPS TO CONSTITUTE EACH INDIVISUAL LIFE FROM BIRTH RIGHTS TO WORKS RIGHTS AND ALSO TO DEATH RIGHTS.AS A CITIZEN I BELIEVE ONE MUST LIVE ACCORDING TO THEIR CONSTITUTION NOT LAW BECAUSE CONSTITUTION AND LAW BOTH ARE DIFFERENT IN NATURE AND RESPECTIVE IMPLEMENTATION . LAW IS FOR CRIMES AND CRIMINALS BUT CONSTITUTION GIVE RIGHTS AND FORCE EVERY INDIVIZUAL TO UNDERSTAND THEIR DUTIES AND RESPONSIBILITIES FOR THEIR NATION AND ALSO GIVE RIGHTS TO AMEND WHENEVER REQUIRE WITH AN ELECTRORAL PROCESS. IF I WANT TO BE AN ENTREPRENEUR I MUST PREFER A MARKET WHERE MAXIMUM PERCENTAGE OF PEOPLE FIRMLY BELIEVE & LIVE ACCORDING TO THEIR CONSTITUTION AND AVOID LAWS IN DAY TO DAY LIFE MANIFESTATION . REMEMBER ONE THING A GOOD ARTICULATED CONSTITUTION HELPS CITIZENS OR USERS TO FOLLOW THEIR DREAMS AND ENCOURAGE CITIZENS TO ACHIEVE THEIR GOALS BUT LAW IS REQUIRE WHEN CITIZENS COMMITTED A CRIME BECAUSE LAW HAS OFFENCE AND DEFENCE CLAUSES. THE CITIZEN WHO BELIEVES IN CONSTITUTION MIGHT BE PART OF A GOOD NATION AND THE CITIZENS WHO BELIVES IN LAWS MIGHT BE A PART OF CRIME NATION. ENTREPRENEUR MADE DREAMS TRUE THROUGH THEIR PRODUCTS WHICH HELP USERS OF NATION MEANS INDIRECTLY BUILT NATION .

HOW TO MAKE LOSS IN BUSINESS

ITS TIME TO FIND OUT THE BEST CONSTITUTION IN TERMS OF FEW ARTICLES , IN TERMS OF EASY MEMORIZE AND IN TERMS OF EASY CHANT , WHEN EVER REQUIRED BY THE PEOPLE ,FOR THE PEOPLE , OF THE PEOPLE AND TO THE PEOPLE OF AN UNIQUE REGION . A HEALTHY CONSTITUTION IS NOT ALL ABOUT 15 TO 20 FEW ARTICLES BUT ITS ALL ABOUT HOW TO DEFINE INDIVISUAL LIFE INTERMS OF LIVE ,RESPECT ,WORK , LEARN ,PEACE, HARMONY, EMPOWER, ENTHUISTIC, ENERGETIC, TRUTH . JUST THINK ABOUT WHEN WE WILL DO BUSINESS IN THIS BEAUTIFUL CONSTITUTIONAL LANGUAGE THEN ONE CAN IMAGINE THAT HOW WOULD BE THE PRODUCT LOOKS LIKE FOR USE . A PRODUCTS WHICH CONTAINS INFORMATION MEANS IT EDUCATE AN USER FOR HEALTHY SURVIVAL .

FREE IMAGES TO UNDERSTAND DREAM ROUTE OF AN ENTREPRENEUR

AS AN AUTHOR OF THIS BOOK " HOW TO MAKE LOSS IN BUSINESS " FIRST OF ALL EYE JUST WANTED TO FEATURED MYSELF INTO AN ENTREPRENEUR CHARACTOR AND WILL TELL ALL USERS HOW TO MAKE LOSS IN BUSINESS STEP BY STEP . IF ANY ONE WANTED TO BE AN ENTREPRENEUR THEN CAN FOLLOW MY STEPS FROM BOTTOM TO ROOF . IF EYE START MY OWN BUISNESS THEN EYE HAVE TO MAKE A LONG VISION MEANS EYE HAVE TO CONVINCED MYSELF FIRST AND HAVE TO CREATE A ROUTE FOR THIS LONG VISION . THE ROUTE MAY BE A BLUR ONE OR MAY BE AN IMAGINARY ONE OR MAY BE A PROJECTED ROUTE WITH ARTIFICIAL FIGURES ONE OR MAY BE A DREAM ROUTE ONE . HERE EYE HAVE TO DEALT WITH COUPLE OF THINGS EITHER

WITH PROFIT OR WITH LOSS , SO NEED TO BE VERY WISE WHILE CHOOSING ROUTE , WISE MEANS HAVING SOUND KNOWLEDGE OF EVERY BUSINESS LANGUAGES . BUSINESS LAGUAGE IS QUITE DIFFERENT FROM CONSTITUTIONAL LANGUAGES .

FREE IMAGES TO UNDERSTAND THE IMAGINARY ROUTE OF AN ENTREPRENEUR

WHEN EYE FINALLY DECIDED TO COMMENCE A BUSINESS ,HERE ALSO EYE HAVE TO CONSTITUTE FEW TERMS AND CONDITIONS TO RUN THE BUSINESS .A TERMS JOURNEY IS ONLY POSSIBLE IF IT MEETS AND GREETS ALL CONDITIONS . IF EYE DEPICT A BUSINESS PICTURE FOR FIRST YEAR TERMS THEN EYE HAVE TO WORK WITH ALL KIND OF PLEASANT ,UNPLEASANT CONDITIONS TO FIGURE OUT A RESULT .IT MAY BE PROFIT OR MAY BE LOSS BUT THERE IS HUGE DIFFERENCE BETWEEN A PROJECTED PROFIT & LOSS BALANCE SHEET AND REAL PROFIT & LOSS BALANCE SHEET . PROJECTED ROUTE ITS KIND OF VISION AND IF WE WORK ACCORDING TO ALL DIFFERENT KIND OF VISION ROUTE ,MAY BE WE GET PROFIT OR MAY BE ENCOUNTERED WITH LOSS . MAY BE IS COMMON WORD IN BUSINSS AND IT USED TO UNDERSTAND THE PROJECTED ACCRUAL ACCOUNTING .

FREE IMAGES OF ACCOUNTABLE BLUR ROUTE OF AN ENTREPRENEUR

ACCOUNTING IS A CHAPTER OF ANY BUSINESS WHICH HELPS TO STREAMLINE A BUSINESS FROM INFORMAL BUSINESS TO FORMAL BUSINESS . AS WE KNOW AND HEARD MANY THING ABOUT BUSINESS BUT ONE THINGS IS COMMON IN ALL TYPE OF BUSINESS THAT BUSINESS HAS MANY DIFFERENT TYPES OF ENTRIES AND EXIT DOORS AND BUSINESS ALWAYS ALLOWS ALL SORT OF ENTRIES BECAUSE BUSINESS HAS VERY CLEAR MESSAGE THAT EVERY ENTRY HAS AN EXIT . IN BUSINESS LANGUAGE ENTRY MEANS INWARD OF CASH ,CHEQUES ,CREDIT SELLS IN TO BUSINESS AND EXIT MEANS OUTWARD OF CASH , CREDIT AND SERVICE AS WELL .

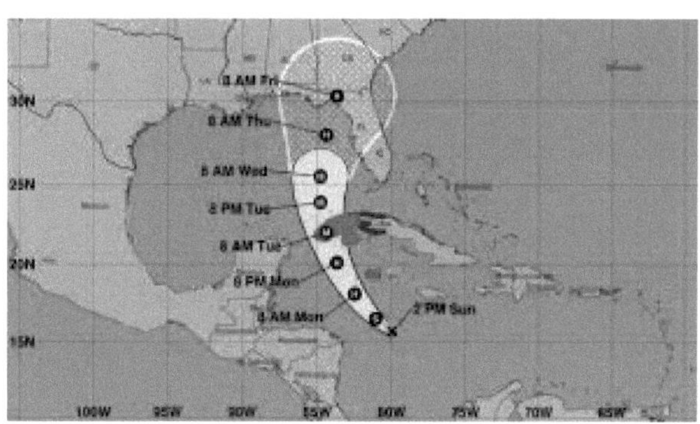

FREE IMAGES FOR UNDERSTANDING THE PROJECTED HURRICANE ROUTE OF AN ENTREPRENEUR

THE BEST THING ABOUT BUSINESS ACCOUNTING THAT IT TAUGHT US A SECURE FINANCIAL FLOW CHART AND IT RECORDS EVERY ENTRIES TO SUBSTANTIATE THE INCORPORATED BUSINESS . IF ANY ENTREPRENUER HAS SOUND KNOWLEDGE ON ACCOUNTS THEN IT EASY TO UNDERSATND AS WELL AS HANDLE THE BUSINESS FOR SMOOTH RUN. EYE BELIEVE ONETHING THAT ,WHEN ANY TRADE HAPPENED IT THROUGH CASH TO GENERATE CASH AND CASH IS THE REAL ACCOUNT IN THIS OVERALL FINANCIAL STRUCTURE . ONLY AN EDUCATED ENTREPRENEUR WILL UNDERSTAND THE SENTIMENT AND EMOTION OF THE BUSINESS MARKET BECAUSE THE PRODUCTS WE MADE THATS EDUCATION , TO FIX A PRICE FOR PRODUCTS THAT ALSO EDUCATION , SEARCH A MARKET TO RETAIL THIS PRODUCTS THATS ALSO PART OF EDUCATION , SO DEVELOP ANY GOOD PRODUCTS IS KIND OF ISM MEANS A COMPREHENSIVE THEORY AND WHEN WE THINK ABOUT TO DEVELOP A NATURAL PRODUCTS LIKE TO DEVELOP AN ISLAND THEN ONETHING CAME INTO OUR MIND THAT WHO WAS OR IS THE ARCHITECT OF THIS NATURAL PRODUCTS BUT WE HAVE SOUND KNOWLEDGE ABOUT THE INVENTOR OF THE PRODUCTS WHICH IS USED BY USERS IN DAY TO DAY LIFE . LETS FIGURED OUT THESE FEW EXAMPLE OF NATURAL PRODUCTS WHICH HAS MADE BY AN UNKNOWN ARCHITECT.

FREE IMAGES OF NATURAL PRODUCTS

FREE IMAGE OF ANOTHER NATURAL PRODUCTS MADE BY AN UNKNOWN ARCHITECT

HOW TO MAKE LOSS IN BUSINESS

IN AN ENTREPRENEUR JOURNEY , 'INVESTMENT' IS ONE OF THE KEY WORD TO UNDERSTAND BECAUSE IN BUSINESS , INVESTMENT MEANS FIRST INVEST ON SELF ,INVEST ON TIME ,INVEST ON PRODUCTS ,INVEST ON RELATION ,INVEST ON MARKET.THE WHOLE CONCEPT OF INVESTMENT TO ENVISAGE A HIKE OF THE WORK PORCESS . WE HUMAN THINKS A LOT AND ALSO WE ARE CAPABLE TO GENERATE MILLIONS OF THOUGHT IN OUR BREATHING JOURNEY BUT IT'S VERY HARD FOR US TO COVERT OUR MILLIONS OF THOUGHTS INTO REALITY. ENVISAGE A BEAUTIFUL PICTURE IN MIND BUT HAS GIVEN LESS EFFORT TO THE PICTURE MEANS WE INVESTED ON FICTION AND THE WORSE THING ABOUT FICTION THAT IT'S DANGEROUS THAN REALITY . FIRST WE HAVE CREATE A CLEAR THOUGHT PROCESS ABOUT PRODUCT BUSINESS, SHALL WE GO FOR A NATURAL PRODUCTS OR MAN MADE PRODUCTS FOR INVESTMENT .AN INVESTOR UNDERSTAND ONLY THE LANUGUAGE MONEY WHICH SUPPOSE TO INVEST ON THE IDEAL PROJECTS OF AN ENTREPRENEUR AND AN ENTREPRENEUR MAY BE AN INVESTOR .

FREE IMAGE OF AN ENTRPRENEUR WHO IS LOOKING FOR AN INVESTOR

FREE IMAGE THE JOURNEY OF ENTREPRENEUR IN ALL DIRECTION

HOW TO MAKE LOSS IN BUSINESS

WHEN WE THINKING ABOUT INVESTMENT THEN WE NEED TO BE VERY CAREFUL ALWAYS BECAUSE INVESTMENT ON GOOD PRODUCTS GIVES US SOUND GROWTH AND THE BOTTOM LINE OF HUMAN JOURNEY IS TO GROW EITHER WITH A NATURAL PRODUCTS OR MAN MADE PRODUCTS IN THIS RENTED LIGHT YEAR LIFE AND THE BEST MEANING OF GROWTH IS ALL ABOUT FACT ,WE LEARN IN ALL DIRECTION . ANY ONE CAN BE AN ENTRPRENEUR BECAUSE THE CONCEPT OF ENTRPRENEUR JOURNEY START FROM ZERO INVESTMENT TO MAXIMUM INVESTMENT . SETTING UP A BUSINESS WITH A GOOD PRODUCT KNOWLEDGE WILL GIVE GOOD RETURN IN TERMS OF MONEY ,IN TERMS OF GROWTH .

AS AN ENTRPRENEUR WHEN EYE STARTED THINKING TO INVEST ON NATURAL PRODUCTS THAN MAN MADE PRODUCTS , WE WILL DISCUSS EVERY PRODUCTS WHICH MEANT FOR INVESTMENT LATER .WHY EYE CHOOSE A NATURAL PRODUCTS FOR AN INVESTMENT ? WHAT IS FACT OF NATURAL PRODUCTS ? LET ME VERY CLEAR ABOUT NATURAL PRODUCTS ,THE FIRST EXAMPLE OF NATURAL PRODUCTS IS TOURISM BECAUSE WE WON'T UNDERSTAND OUR OWN TOUR THEN IT'S VERY DIFFICULT TO UNDERSTAND OTHER PRODUCTS TOUR .WHEN EYE HAVE DECIDED TO INVEST ON NATURAL PRODUCTS THEN EYE FIGURED OUT THAT INVEST ON TOURISM PRODUCTS IS ONE OF THE BEST OPTION TO SUBSTANTIATE THE BREATHING LIFE ON EARTH .

FREE IMAGE OF WATER FALLS A NATURAL PRODUCTS

FREE IMAGE OF ISLAND A NATURAL PRODUCTS

FREE IMAGE OF HILL STATION A NATURAL PRODUCTS

WHEN WE EQUIPPED WITH NATURE AND IF EYE BELIVE IF EYE INVEST ON THESE NATURAL PRODUCTS THEN THERE WOULD BE A LESS CHANCES OF LOSS BUT CAN DEPICT A PRO FIT FOR A PROFIT .

HOW TO MAKE LOSS IN BUSINESS

AS AS ENTREPRENEUR ,EYE BELIEVE INVESTMENT ON NATURAL TOURISM PRODUCTS MEANS IF EYE SUCCEED THEN EYE DEFINITELY WOULD BE AN INSPIRATION FOR OTHER ENTREPRENEURS BUT IF EYE FAIL THEN EYE GET HUGE LESSON ABOUT NATURE ,IT ALSO A PART OF ASSETS. TO CREATE ASSET WITH NATURAL PRODUCTS MEANS TO ENHANCE KNOWLEDGE WHICH HAS ONLY APPRECIATION IN HUMAN FIXED ASSET CALCULATION. AS AN AUTHOR'S POINT OF VIEW , EYE DESCRIBED THE NATURAL TOURISM PRODUCTS AS SOURCE OF MY CREATIVITY BECAUSE AS AS AUTHOR EYE ENVIAGE A QUITE DIFFERENT VIEW THEN AN ENTREPRENEUR VIEW ABOUT ONE OF THE NATURAL PRODCTS "AN ISLAND " . IF SOMEBODY ASK ME , MY VIEW ON ISLANDS THEN IN SIMPLE WORDS FIRST EYE PAY RESPECT TO THE UNKNOWN ARCHITECT WHO DESIGNED AND CREATED THIS WONDER . EITHER THIS UNKNOWN ARCHITECT WAS A LOVER AND DID FOR HER LOVE BECAUSE AS AN AUTHOR'S PERSPECTIVE, AN ISLAND IS A PLACE WHERE FEMALE READY TO OPEN AND ALLOW LOVER TO TOUCH HER ,A FEMALE ALWAYS FEEL SECURED WITH HER MALE IN SUCH KIND OF PLACES WHICH CUT OFF FROM MAINLAND AND THE LAND WHICH SURROUNDED WITH THE COLORFUL WATER OF OCEAN .

FREE IMAGES EXAMPLE OF CREATING NEW GENERATION

AN ISLAND IS A KIND OF PLACE WILL FORCE ANYONE TO RETHINK ABOUT THE GENERATION THEY ALL HAVE ALREADY BEEN THROUGH AND ALSO PROVE THEM WRONG . IF YOU ARE READY TO SQUARE UP IN AN ISLAND THEN YOU WILL BE FELT LIKE ,THE FIRST ORIGIN OF HUMAN CREATION . THE REASON TO BELIEVE THAT EYE DON'T HAVE CLEAR RECORD ABOUT THE HISTORY OF ANY ISLAND . NOW AS AN ENTREPRENEUR'S PERSPECTIVE IF EYE INVEST ON THIS ISLAND THEN FIRST EYE HAVE TO UNDERSTAND THE HUMAN NATURE AND THE BEHAVIOUR TOWARDS THESE TOURISM PLACES BECAUSE HUMANS IN EARTH ARE ONE OF THE FINEST VERSION OF NATURAL TOURISM PRODUCTS.

FREE IMAGE ABOUT FINEST EXAMPLE OF NATURAL TOURISM PRODUCTS

HOW TO MAKE LOSS IN BUSINESS

WHEN WE INVESTEED ON NATURAL TOURISM PRODUCTS THEN WE HAVE TO BE MORE CAREFUL ABOUT THE NATURAL CONSEQUENCES , IN SIMPLE LANGUAGE THAT OUR NATURE HAS MANY SIDES AND WE ONLY ACKNOWLEDGE FEW SIDES OF NATURE LIKE THE POSITIVE AND THE NEGATIVE SIDES . AS AN ENTREPRENEUR IF EYE FULLY INVEST MY ENERGY ON NATURAL TOURISM PRODUCTS THEN ONE BIGGEST FACT WILL COME OUT AND THAT WOULD BE ONLY A VERY CLEAR BALANCE SHEET OF ASSETS AND LIABILITIES. AS A HUMAN , EYE KNOW THAT MY JOURNEY IS WITH NATURE AND TO UNDERTAND NATURE, ONLY TO SCREW OUR MIND BECAUSE THE NATURAL TOURISM PRODUCTS LIKE ISLANDS ,HILL ,WATERFALLS ,HUMAN MALE ,FEMALE SUN,MOON ,STARS ,RAIN, SNOWFALLS AND MANY MORE THINGS, ALL HAS DARK SECRETS AND WE HAVE TO REDICOVER THE HISTORY OF THESE THINGS. AS AN AUTHOR EYE HAVE A STRONG BELIEVE ON MY WRITTEN WORDS THAT REAL HISTORY OR REAL TRUTH HAS BEEN BURIED BY OUR ANCERSTORS . AS A HUMAN, FIRST EYE HAVE TO DIG OUT THE FACT OF EARTH WHICH HAS BEEN BURIED AND HAVE TO CREATE ANXIETY AMONG PEOPLE FOR NATURAL TOURISM PRODUCTS.

HOW ISLAND FORMED ?

HERE WE NEED TO UNDERSTAND ONE THINGTHAT ,WE ARE NOT PART OF A REAL HISTORY IN TERMS OF TRUTH . AN ISLAND IS ALSO KNOWN AS A DESERTED PLACE .

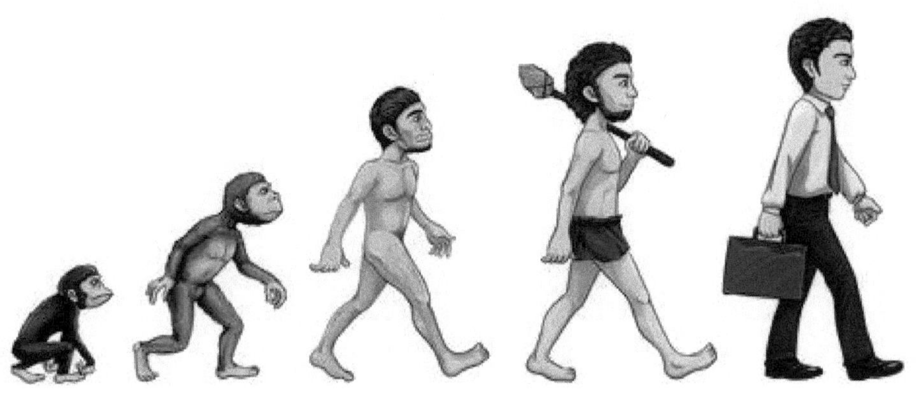

FREE IMAGE TO FIGURE OUT THE FACT OF THIS HUMAN EVOLUTION

IS IT POSSIBLE TO FIGURED OUT THE REAL TRUTH OF THIS HUMAN EVOLUTION IN THIS THOUSAND YEARS OF JOURNEY ? YES BUT THE REAL ANSWER IS NO OR IMPOSSIBLE. BUT WE CAN RE-DISCOVER FEW REAL TRUTH IN THIS HUMAN TOUR BY USING INTELLIGENCE AND WITH WIT . EVERY DAY WE SEE STARS ,SUN , MOON IN OUR NAKED EYES BUT WE STILL DON'T , HOW OUR EYES TRAVERSE THROUGH THIS BILLIONS OF MILES ? IN FACT NO BODY TAUGHT US THAT HUMAN EYE ARE SYNCHRONIZED WITH LIGHT AND STILL WE DON'T WHO NAMED LIGHT "SUN" , DEEM LIGHT " MOON" AND THE SPARK LIGHT "STARS ". THE MOST INTERESTING FACT OF ALL HUMAN IF ANYONE ASK THEM ABOUT THIER ONLY 250 YEARS FAMILY HISTORY THEN THE REAL ANSWER IS DON'T KNOW BUT ASK THEM TELL SOME STORIES ABOUT JESUS , ALLAH, HINDU GOD AND GODDES , AND BUDDHA THEN DEFINITELY GET SOME POSSITIVE ANSWERS AS IF THEY BELONG TO THIS ERA . EYE WAS THINKING ABOUT THE REGION,THE SPOKEN LANGUAGES BUT STILL NEVER UNDERSTAND THE RELIGION , WHEREAS THIS RELIGION CLAIMED THAT THEY EXISTS MORE THAN THOUSAND YEARS. AS WE KNOW OUR EARTH HAS MANY SPOKEN LANGUAGES OF MANY DIFFERENT REGION THEN HOW CAN WE FIGURE OUT ONE THAT YES , THIS IS OLDEST LAGUAGE OF THOUSANDS OF SPOKEN LANGUAGES .

FREE IMAGE OF DIFFERENT SPOKEN LANGUAGES OF EARTH

AS AN AUTHOR OF THIS BOOK " HOW TO MAKE LOSS IN BUSINESS " ,IF EYE GET AN OPPORTUNITY TO CREATE A NEW SPOKEN LANGUAGE AND DEVELOP THE LANGUAGE FOR DAY TO DAY COOMUNICATION THEN EYE CAN BUILT A LANGUAGE OF MINIMUM 17 LETTERS TO MAXIMUM 21 LETTERS WHERE ONE CAN GET VOWELS AND CONSONANTS AND EYE BELIEVE THIS WOULD BE RECOMMEND FOR GUNIESS BOOK OF WORLD RECORDS. AN ALPHABET OF ONLY 17 LETTERS FOR READING ,WRITING,LISTENING AND ALSO FOR SPEAKING . ONE CAN EASILY MEMORIZE 17 LETTERS ALPHABET AND TONES FOR PRONOUNCIATION .

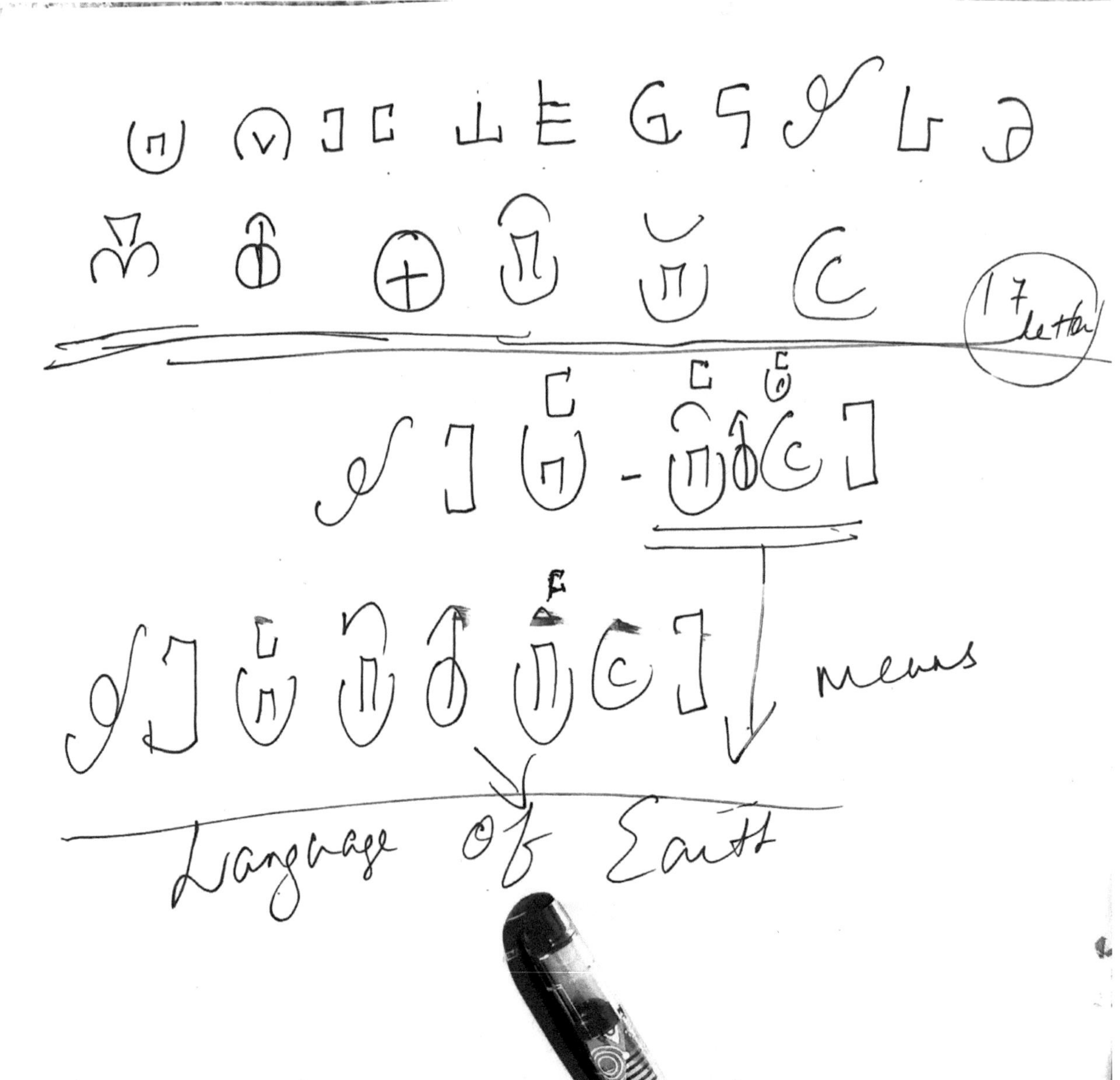

IMAGE OF NEW SPOKEN LANGUAGE WHICH HAS BEEN CREATED BY ME

HOW TO MAKE LOSS IN BUSINESS

IF EYE STARTED WRITING MY EMOTION, MY THOUGHTS , MY VISION IN MY OWN CREATED 17 LETTERS ALPHABET LANGUAGE THEN EVEN ITS VERY DIFFICULT FOR GOOGLE -ALPHABET TO TRANSLATE MY BOOK IN TO OTHER LANGUAGE WITHOUT ME . FIRST TO UNDERSTAND WHY SO MANY DIFFERENT LANGUAGES IN ONE EARTH AND WHY NOT ONE EARTH ONE LANGUAGE CONCEPT . IF EYE INVEST ON THIS LANGUAGE PROJECT THEN IT'S KIND OF LENDING TO SELF MEANS LOAN TO SELF AND MUTUALLY SHARED THE INTEREST .EYE WILL GIVE A FINEST EXAMPLE ,KINDLY HANG ON TO THIS SMALL STORY

FREE IMAGE OF LOAN TO SELF ON NEW CREATED ALPHABET LANGUAGE PROJECT

a story teller also have poetic heart when thinks about real poetry . Small story ,the journey of A guy name sarbeswar (the name Given by me) and his action on auction .when eye follow this guy ,its real incredible ,neither manipulated nor articulated . sarbeswar journey with a loan of 5,00,000. Its seems like amorphous but this is one kind of loan that sarbeswar is not going to amortize the debt . Loan is asset part ,the institute who has given loan amount to sarbeswar ,neither asking for repayment of the loan amount .

I am really shocked ,a guy (ME) followed sarbeswar for his steps now a question screwing my mind what will happen to sarbeswar in the next phase of his life .sarbeswar means a lot with its name ,it sabu +eswar means God , this name blessed with god .

This story teller has a G+7 storyed attitude . And G+7 means a figure of 8 .and 8 means very close to cloud 9 .

IMAGE OF THE FIRST PROMOTER OF ANY NEW ALPHABET LANGUAGE

IF EYE CREATED A NEW ALPHABET LANGUAGE FOR COMMUNICATION THEN EYE MUST FIND OUT SOME ONE MEANS A FEMALE TO PROMULGATE MY NEW ALPHABET BECAUSE A FEMALE IS ONLY OPTION , THE WAY SHE CARRY A KID FOR SEVERAL MONTHS AND AFTER DELIVERED TO THE WORLD , THIS KID PROBABLY WOULD BE THE FASTEST LEARNER AS WELL AS THE FIRST SPEAKER OF THIS NEW LANGUAGE EVEN WITHOUT UNDERSTANDING OF ANY LETTERS OF ALPHABET . THIS IS THE KIND OF INTELLECTUAL RELATION BETWEEN A MOTHER AND HER KID AND THATS ONLY THE REASON THE KID UNDERSTAND THE MOTHER'S LANGUAGE .

HOW TO MAKE LOSS IN BUSINESS

WHEN EYE THINK TO INVEST MY INTEREST ON MY NEW ALPHABET LANGUAGE PROJECT FOR FUTURE COMMUNICATION THEN EYE NEED TO BE VERY FOCUSED ON MY VISION BECAUSE IT'S NOT THATEASY TO SPREAD A NEW LANGUAGE ACROSS REGION ,ACROSS GLOBE .LANGUAGE IS SOMETHING LIKE HELP TO BUILT A COMMUNITY ,HELP TO BUILT A REGION ,HELP TO BUILT BEHAVIOUR AND MANY MORE THINGS FOR A BETTER EARTH. LANGUAGE IS CALLED A MANMADE PRODUCTS AND EYE THINK TO AGAIN PROMOTE LANGUAGE TOURISM THEN EYE MUST HAVE TO GO THROUGH THE PAST ,PRESENT SPOKEN LANGUAGES OF GLOBE. IF EYE USE MY NEW LANGUAGE FOR TRADE THEN EYE HAVE NOTHING PURCHASE ,JUST TO SELL THE LETTERS OF ALPHABET AND EYE DON'T THING ANY HUGE FINANCIAL INVESTMENT REQUIRE TO ACCOMPLISH THE LANGUAGE TOURISM PROJECTS . ANY ONE IN THIS EARTH WHO WANT TO DEVELOP THIS KIND OF PROJECTS , MEANS WANT TO SEE THE INTELLECTUAL PEOPLE IN A SINGLE PLATFORM . LANGUAGE IS AN INTELLECTUAL PRODUCTS , EVERY DAY THESE PEOPLE WILL INVENT NEWWORDS FROM THESE NEW LETTERS . IT'S A HUGE INVESTMENT ON PEOPLE BY ANY STARTUP ENTREPRENEUR.

FREE IMAGE OF CONNECTED WORLD FOR TRADE ONLY

AS WE KNOW THAT NOW WE LIVE IN SUCH A WORLD WHERE LIFE MEANS BUSINESS OR TRADE .EACH AND EVERYDAY WE BUY PRODUCTS FOR OUR USE BUT THE SELLER WHO SOLD THE PRODUCTS TO BUYER HAS AN UNIQUE ACCOUNT OF TRADE ,PROFIT & LOSS AND HAS TO BALANCE ALL OF THESE ACCOUNT FOR TAXATION . WE ALL KNOW LETTER "T " IS THE FORMAT OF TRADE , AN UNIQUE SIGN OF BUYING AND SELLING .

FREE IMAGE OF NATURAL T SHAPE TRADE TOURISM PRODUCTS

BUT TRADE ON NATURAL TOURISM PRODUCTS IS SOMETHING DIFFRENT FROM OTHER PRODUCTS ,HERE EYE HAVE TO ONLY PURCHASE THE NEEDS AND REQUIREMENTS OF INDIVIZUALS AS WELL AS GROUPS . HERE ONLY EYE HAVE TO DISTINGUISH THING TO CREATE EXCITEMENT AMONG CLIENTS AND THE NATURE LOVERS AND TO CREATE A UNIQUE SELLING POINT OF A NATURAL TOURISM PRODCTS BY THOROUGH RESEARCH . SOMTIMES WE HUNT THE PAST ANCIENT HISTORY FOR A REAL TRUTH BECAUSE OF THIS UNIVERSAL TRUTH OF HUMAN " BORN TO DIE ONE DAY" . IN NATURAL TOURISM PRODUCTS FIRST TO UNDERSTAND WHO AM I AND MY LIVING POSITION IN EARTH WITH RESPECT TO LIGHT. AS AS AUTHOR AND ALSO IN AN ENTREPRENEUR JOURNEY WHEN EYE FIGURED OUT POSIYION OF SELF IN 5.30 G.M.T THEN EYE STARTED THINKING ABOUT THE OTHERS POSITION WHO ARE SITTING AT POSTITIVE INTEGERS TO NEGATIVE INTEGERS OF G.M.T AND THE BEST INCREDIBLE THING ABOUT G.M.T WHICH EYE HAVE FERRETED OUT THE FUTURE TIME ,PRESENT TIME AND THE PAST TIME IN THIS 24HOURS ,WHEN EYE GET UP AT 8 O' CLOCK MORNRIG WITH THE REMARK OF PRESENT TIME AND IN THE SAME TIME THOSE WHO SAT IN POSITIVE INTEGERS OF G.M.T WOULD HAVE LIVED WITH A REMARK OF GOOD AFTERNOON . MY FUTURE TIME WITH THEIR PRESENT TIME . WITH THIS EXTRAORDINARY FACT , EYE WAS THINKING TO INVEST ON MY NEARES T POSTIVE INTEGER G.M.T BECAUSE IF START WITH POSITIVE VIDES THEN MAY WE GET A POITIVE RESULTS. THE BEST THING ABOUT NATURAL TOURISM PRODUCTS THAT WE DON'T NEED TO GO THROUGH THESE BUSINESS LANGUAGES. HERE TRADE MEANS RESEARCH AND REDISCOVER THINGS WHICH BASED ON TRUTH .

HOW TO MAKE LOSS IN BUSINESS

INVEST ON NATURAL TOURISM PRODUCTS ,FIRST TO SET UP A TRAVEL AND TOUR OPERATION AGENCY FOR NATURAL TOURISM PRODUCTS EXPLORATION AND HERE ONE THING IS COMMON LIKE OTHER TRADES I.E BUY AND SELL BUT THE BEST THING ABOUT TOURISM TRADE TOUR OPERATION THAT IT NEVER EVER WILL THROUGH THIS TRADING LANGUAGES LIKE CARRIAGE INWARDS ,TRANSPORTATION INWARDS,FREIGHT INWARDS , ANY INSURANCE IN TRANSIT , WAGES , EXERCISE DUTIES ON MANUFACTURING BECAUSE HERE NOTHING TO MANUFACTURE ,CLEARING CHARGES , DOCK CHARGES , COAL ,COKE ,GAS , FUEL , FACTORY POWER OIL ,WATER FACTORY EXPENSES , OCTROI ,COMMISION ON PURCHASE , SHIPPING EXPENSES ON PURCHASE . JUST OPEN WITH BALANCE AND GET TO KNOW THE PURCHASE ONLY BASIS OF SALE . HERE IN TRAVEL AND TOUR OPERATION BUSINESS ONLY HAVE TO PURCHASE THE DAYS AND NIGHTS. NATUARAL TOURISM RESOURCES ARE THERE ONLY TO EXPLORE THROUGH WIT . IN TRADE WHEN CASH IS DEBITED FOR ANY TYPE OF PURCHASE LIKE FURNITURE , COMPUTER , SOFTWARE, MOTOR CAR TO RUN AN OFFICE ,OFTEN CALLED AN ASSET BUT WE CAN GENERATE REVEUNE BY THE PROPER USE OF THESE ASSET ND WHEN WE CREDITED THE SALES MEANS THE DEVELOPED PRODUCT GET RECOGNIZED AND AWARDED , THE TAGGED PRICE CREDITED THROUGH SALES AND IT GIVES US IMMENSE PLEASURE BECAUSE THE PRODUCTS WE EXPLORE HAS FINALLY BEEN PAID . WHEN WE CHOOSE A NATURAL TOURISM PRODUCTS THERE MUST BE SOMETHING TO LEARN .

FREE IMAGE OF ZODIAC SIGN

मेष	Aries	चू	चे	चो	ला	ली	लू	ले	लो	अ
व्रष	Taurus	इ	उ	ए	ओ	वा	वी	वू	वे	वो
मिथुन	Gemini	का	की	कू	घ	ड़	छ	के	को	हा
कर्क	Cancer	ही	हू	हे	हो	डा	डी	डू	डे	डो
सिंह	Leo	मा	मी	मु	मे	मो	टा	टी	टू	टे
कन्या	Virgo	टो	पा	पी	पु	ष	ण	ठ	पे	पो
तुला	Libra	रा	री	रु	रे	रो	ता	ती	तू	ते
वृश्चिक	Scorpio	तो	ना	नी	नू	ने	नो	या	यी	यू
धनु	Sagittarius	ये	यो	भा	भी	भू	ध	फ	ढ	भे
मकर	Capricorn	भो	जा	जी	खी	खू	खे	खो	गा	गी
कुम्भ	Aquarius	गू	गे	गो	सा	सी	सू	से	सो	दा
मीन	Pisces	दी	दू	थ	झ	ञ	दे	दो	चा	ची

FREE IMAGE OF INDIAN ZODIAC SIGN NAMES

2023
CALENDAR THAILAND

มกราคม

						1
2	3	4	5	6	7	8
9	10	11	12	13	14	15
16	17	18	19	20	21	22
23	24	25	26	27	28	29
30	31					

กุมภาพันธ์

		1	2	3	4	5
6	7	8	9	10	11	12
13	14	15	16	17	18	19
20	21	22	23	24	25	26
27	28					

มีนาคม

		1	2	3	4	5
6	7	8	9	10	11	12
13	14	15	16	17	18	19
20	21	22	23	24	25	26
27	28	29	30	31		

เมษายน

					1	2
3	4	5	6	7	8	9
10	11	12	13	14	15	16
17	18	19	20	21	22	23
24	25	26	27	28	29	30

พฤษภาคม

1	2	3	4	5	6	7
8	9	10	11	12	13	14
15	16	17	18	19	20	21
22	23	24	25	26	27	28
29	30	31				

มิถุนายน

			1	2	3	4
5	6	7	8	9	10	11
12	13	14	15	16	17	18
19	20	21	22	23	24	25
26	27	28	29	30		

กรกฎาคม

					1	2
3	4	5	6	7	8	9
10	11	12	13	14	15	16
17	18	19	20	21	22	23
24	25	26	27	28	29	30
31						

สิงหาคม

	1	2	3	4	5	6
7	8	9	10	11	12	13
14	15	16	17	18	19	20
21	22	23	24	25	26	27
28	29	30	31			

กันยายน

				1	2	3
4	5	6	7	8	9	10
11	12	13	14	15	16	17
18	19	20	21	22	23	24
25	26	27	28	29	30	

ตุลาคม

						1
2	3	4	5	6	7	8
9	10	11	12	13	14	15
16	17	18	19	20	21	22
23	24	25	26	27	28	29
30	31					

พฤศจิกายน

		1	2	3	4	5
6	7	8	9	10	11	12
13	14	15	16	17	18	19
20	21	22	23	24	25	26
27	28	29	30			

ธันวาคม

				1	2	3
4	5	6	7	8	9	10
11	12	13	14	15	16	17
18	19	20	21	22	23	24
25	26	27	28	29	30	31

FREE IMAGES OF THAI LANGUAGE CALENDER

EYE DON'T KNOW WHO NAMED INDIAN ZODIAC SIGN , NAMED ENGLISH ZODIAC SIGN AND NAMED THAI MONTHS NAME BUT WE WILL GET A HUGE IDEOLOGICAL DIFFERENCE IN THESE ABOVE IMAGES IN LANGUAGE TOUR . AS AS AUTHOR OF THIS BOOK " HOW TO MAKE LOSS IN BUSINESS " EVEN EYE HAVE BEEN TRYING TO UNDERSTAND THE IDEOLOGICAL DIFFERENCES OF DIFFERENT TIME ZONES FOR MANY YEARS . WHY THIS SIMILAR SOUND NAMES AND WHAT HAD HAPPENED AT ANCIENT EARTH ? SO MANY QUESTIONS BUT STILL NIL ANSWERS OF MY QUESTIONS .

HOW TO MAKE LOSS IN BUSINESS

AS A TRAVEL & TOURISM PROFESIONAL EYE GOT A BEST ANCIENT CHAPTER TO UNDERSTAND AD GET RESEARCH THE PAST ANCIENT CULTURES OF ANCIENT HUMANS. IF ANY ONE WILL LEAF THROUGH THIS TOURISM DATA THEN IT FORCE THEM FOR MORE TRUTH CULTIVATION . IN INDIA HERE MAXIMUM PERCENTAGE OF PEOPLE FIRMLY BELIEVE ON ZODIAC SIGN AND THE IMPACT ON THEIR DAY TO DAY LIFE BUT WHEN GOT TO KNOW THAT THE SAME IDENTICAL NAMES USED AS MONTHS NAME IN A DIFFERENT TIME ZONE OF GLOBE THEN IT WILLBLOW THEM OUT . AS WE KNOW WE ALL HUMAN LIVE IN A CIRCLE OF DARKNESS BUT IDENTIFIED ONLY BY THE LIGHT WITH ITS RESPECTIVE TIME. THIS IS A KIND OF SUBJECT WHICH FORCE ME TO DEVELOP FOR THE WELFARE OF THE PEOPLE AND ALSO FOR THE TOURISM. EVEN IT'S VERY HARD FOR ME TO FIGURED OUT THESE KIND OF SIMILAR WORDS USED IN DIFFERENT TIME ZONE . THE TIME ZONE EYE RESIDE HAS MANY SPOKEN LANGUAGES AND EYE AM CAPABLE TO MENTION UNDERSTAND ONLY COUPLE OF LANGUAGES ,ONE IS MY NATIVE LANGUAGE AND THE SECOND ONE MY NATIONAL LANGUAGE AND APART FROM THAT EYE UNDERSTAND THREE MORE INTERNATIONAL LANGUAGES.

FREE IMAGES OF DIFFERENT LANGUAGES WITH DIFFERENT CULTURES

ONLY THING EYE CAN ASSUME IN MY NAKED EYES THAT THE NUMBER OF SPOKEN LANGUAGES MEANS THE SAME NUMBER OF CULTURES MUST EXIST IN THIS INNER CIRCLE OF DARKNESS WHERE LIGHT IS ONLY WITNESS OF ANCIENT TO FUTURE AND TO RE -PRESENT THE PRESENT.EYE NEVER WANT TO MISS THIS KIND OPPORTUNITY WHICH HAS GIVEN BY THE NATURE TO EXPLORE THE NATURE IN A BROADER HORIZON. SOMETIMES INVEST EVERYTHING ON A DESTINATION WHICH LOCATED AHEAD OF CURRENT DESTINATION IS AN ANOTHER HIGHEST LEVEL OF EXPERIENCE . AS WE KNOW TOURISM IS A VAST SUBJECT TO FINISHED UP WITHIN LIMITED TIME . LETS BEGIN TO UNDERSTAND THE PROCESS OF TRAVEL AGENCY AND TOUR OPERATION STEP BY STEP TO ENVISAGE A HUGE PROFIT.

FREE IMAGE OF TRAVEL INSTRUMENTS TO VOYAGE

IN THIS TRAVEL AGENCY AND OUT BOUND TOUR OPERATION BUSINESS WE HAVE TO DEAL WITH AIRLINES ,TRAINS, BUS , LANGUAGE, HOTELS , VISA, FOREIGN CURRENCY ,TAXIS , PUBLIC TRANSPORTS TO ATTAINED AN OVERSEAS TOUR .SETTING UP TRAVEL & TOUR OPERATION IS VERY EASY BUT FOR A SUSTAINABLE TOURISM DEVELOPMENT , WE HAVE TO CHOOSE AN UNIQUE NATURAL TOURISM PRODUCTS AND HAVE TO BE ACCOUNTABLE FOR THIS PRODUCTS. FOR EXAMPLE IF EYE DEVELOPED A TOURISM PRODUCTS THEN IT MUST RELATED TO THE NATURE LIKE REAL TIME SATELLITE BASED WALKING TOURISM CONCEPT .

FREE IMAGE OF RESERVATION TO SUBSTANTIATE THE TOURISM CONCEPT

WHEN WE ARE LOOKING FOR RESERVATION OF AIR ,HOTEL , TRAIN , BUS ,HOTEL,TAXI CAR THEN WE FOLLOWED AND ALLOWED LIMITED ENTRIES TO OUR BUSINESS . TRAVEL AND TOUR OPERATION IS A KIND OF BUSINESS WHERE ONE CAN EASILY MANTAIN THE FINANCIAL RECORDS OF A COMPANY. IN BUSINESS IT'S ALWAYS NECESSARY TO RECORD ALL TRASACTIONS AS WELL AS RECORD ALL ENTRIES IN A BOOK FOR HEALTHY FINANCIAL COMMUNICATION.TO UNDERSTAND ANY BUSINESS , FIRST ONE HAS TO UNDERSTAND THE FINANCIAL MODULE WHETHER IT'S SMALL ENTREPRENEURSHIP , MEDIUM ENTREPRENEURSHIP OR A BIG ENTREPRENEURSHIP. A SMALL INVESTMENT CAN GIVE HUGE MARGIN OF PROFIT AND A HUGE INVESTMENT MAY BE SETTLED WITH LOW MARGIAN OF LOSS . NOW A DAYS IN MODERN ECONOMY THE CRADLE OF ACCOUNTING BASED ON MODERN CRADLE ACCOUNTING THEORY LIKE C FOR CAPITAL , R FOR REVENUE ,A FOR ASSETS ,D FOR DRAWINGS, L FOR LIABILITIES AND E FOR EXPENSES. WHEN WE TALK ABOUT CAPITAL ,IT MAY BE OWN ,OR MAY BE BORROWED . CAPITAL IS IMPORTANT PART OF BUSINESS TO CREATE ASSETS BUT WE HAVE TO UNDERSTAND CAPITAL ALWAYS A LIABILITY SIDE OF A COMPANY BALANCE SHEET . THE WONDER THING ABOUT THE CAPITAL ACCOUNT ,IT'S KIND OF A RESERVE FUND WHERE WE ADD NET PROFIT IF COMPANY MADE AND LESS THE DRAWINGS BUT STILL IT'S A LIABILITY FOR ANY COMPANY.

HOW TO MAKE LOSS IN BUSINESS

IN ANY BUSINESS THERE WOULD BE A CHANCES OF INCREASE IN ASSETS OR DECREASE IN ASSETS ,INCREASE IN REVENUE OR DECREASE IN REVENUE ,INCREASE IN CAPITAL OR DECREASE IN CAPITAL ,INCREASE IN DRAWINGS OR DECREASE IN DRAWINGS ,INCREASE IN LIABILITIES OR DECREASE IN LIABILITIES .INCREASE IN EXPENSES OR DECRESAE IN EXPENSES AND THIS WHOLE MECHANISM BASED ON THE PRODUCTS IN TERMS OF PRICE ,IN TERMS OF SERVICE AND IN TERMS OF QUALITY . AS AN AUTHOR OF THIS BOOK" HOW TO MAKE LOSS IN BUSINESS" ,USED TO WRITE IN ENGLISH CAPITAL LETTERS FORMAT TO FIGURED OUT THE REST SMALL LETTERS FORMAT AND 2 MORE FORMATS OF WRITING ENGLISH AND STILL EYE NEVER UNDERSTAND WHY THIS ENGLISH LANGUAGE ALPHABET HAS DIFFERENT DESIGN LETTERS FORMAT BECAUSE AS A NATIVE SPEAKER OF ODIA LANGUAGE , WE DO NOT HAVE ANY CAPITAL AND SMALL LETTERS JOURNEY AND EVEN OTHER INTERNATIONAL LANGUAGES ALSO DOESN'T HAVE ANY CAPITAL AND SMALL LETTERS HISTORY.

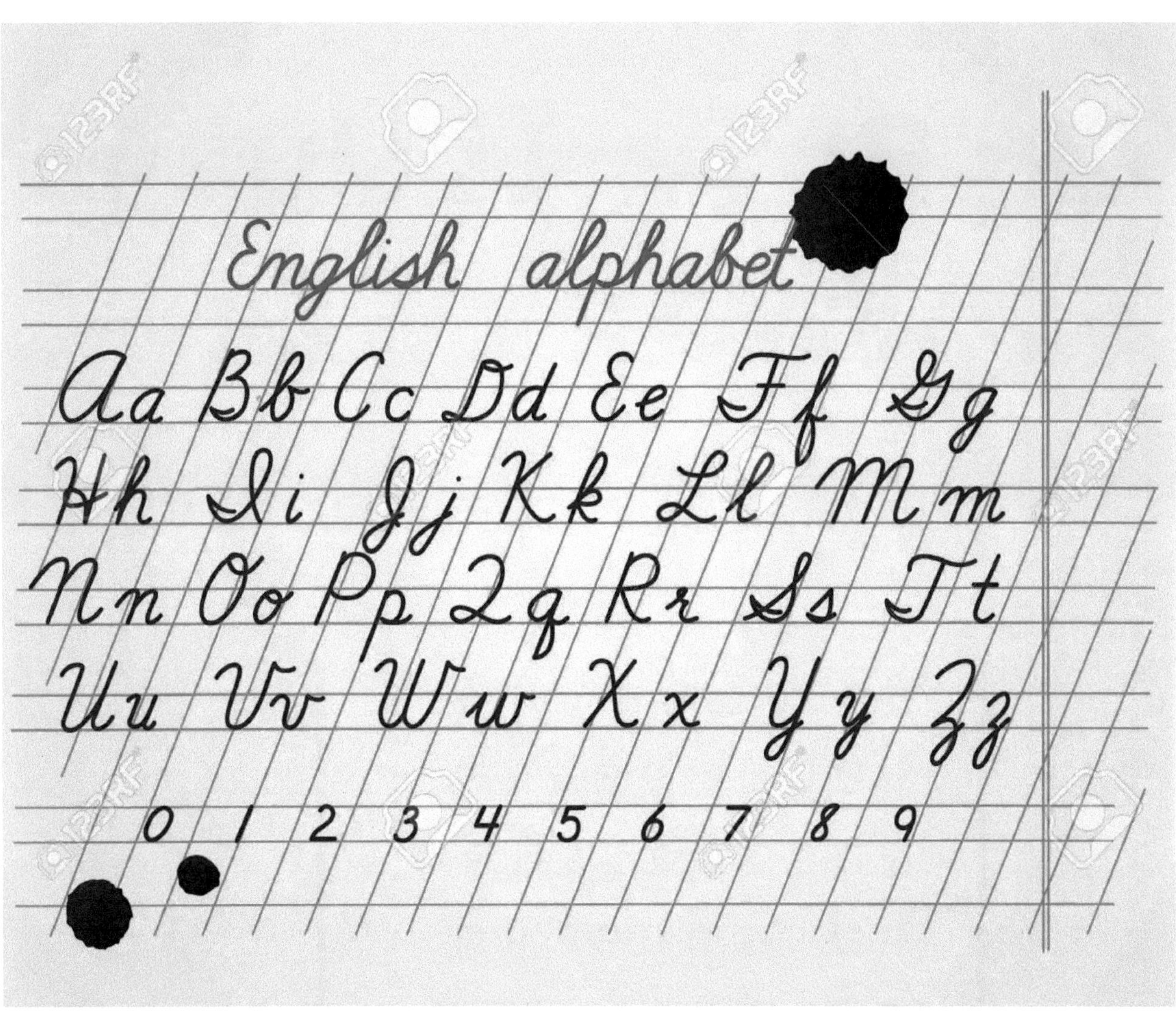

FREE IMAGE OF ENGLISH SMALL ALPHABET FORAMAT

Aa Bb Cc Dd Ee
Ff Gg Hh Ii Jj Kk
Ll Mm Nn Oo Pp
Qq Rr Ss Tt Uu
Vv Ww Xx Yy Zz

FREE IMAGE OF CAPITAL LETTER FORMAT

ଅ ଆ ଇ ଈ ଉ ଊ ଋ ଏ ଐ ଓ ଔ
କ ଖ ଗ ଘ ଙ ଚ ଛ ଜ ଝ ଞ
ଟ ଠ ଡ ଢ ଣ ତ ଥ ଦ ଧ ନ
ପ ଫ ବ ଭ ମ ଯ ର ଲ ଶ ଷ
ସ ହ ଡ଼ ଢ଼ ୟ ଳ କ୍ଷ ଂ ଃ ଁ

FREE IMAGE OF ODIA ALPHABET

FREE IMAGE OF HINDI ALPHABET

ก ข ฃ ค ฅ ฆ ง จ

ฉ ช ซ ฌ ญ ฎ ฏ ฐ

ฑ ฒ ณ ด ต ถ ท ธ

น บ ป ผ ฝ พ ฟ ภ

ม ย ร ล ว ศ ษ ส

ห ฬ อ ฮ

FREE IMAGE OF THAI ALPHABET

Lao Consonants Alphabets/Letters

ພາສາລາວ

ກ ຂ ຄ ງ ຈ

ສ ຊ ຍ ດ ຕ

ຖ ທ ນ ບ ປ

ຜ ຝ ພ ຟ ມ

ຢ ລ ວ ຫ ອ

ຮ ຣ

FREE IMAGE OF LAO ALPHABET

LOOK AT THE BEAUTY OF LANGUAGE TOUR,ENGLIGH STARTS ITS TOUR WITH CAPITAL LETTER AND END UP WITH SMALL LETTER AND STILL EYE AM LOOKING FOR SOMEONE TO GET RESEARCH

ON THIS BEAUTIFUL LAGUAGE TOUR THAT WHAT THE REASON BEHIND THIS CAPITAL AND SMALL LETTER JOURNEY OF ENGLIGH AND WHY OTHER LANGUAGES HAS ONLY FORMAT ,EVEN EYE STILL CONFUSED TO ADDRESS THESE ALPHABET LETTERS , ITS CAPITAL OR SMALL THESE ARE THE PART OF REALTIME SATELLITE BASED WALKING TOURISM PROMOTION. FOR A SUSTAINABLE TOURISM DEVELOPMENT WE NEED TO WORK ON THIS DIFFERENT UNSOLVED LETTERS OF APHABET EQUATION. WHEN WE DEVEOLP GOOD TOURISM PRODUCTS IT HELP US TO INCREASE OUR COMPLANY ASSETS AS WELL AS REVENUE AND DECREASE OUR LIABILITIES , DRAWINGS AND EXPENSES.

EXAMPLE OF GOOD TOURISM PRODUCTS : WALKING TOURISM

IN A HIGHLY SPACE DEVELOPMENT WORLD ,IT'S NECESSARY TO INTRODUCE THIS KIND OF PRODUCTS . AS WE KNOW ALL HUMANS DEVELOPMENT IN EARTH WITH RENTED NATURAL RIGHT YEARS, THIS WALKING TOURISM CONCEPT IS TO KNOW THEMSELVES AND THE PURPOSE OF THEIR LIFE IN LIFE .IN THIS CONCEPT TRAVELLERS ENCOUNTERED AND WITNESS THEIR LIFE WITH INFINTY SPACE WITHOUT VISITING SPACE STATION . IN THIS WALKING TOURISM CONCEPT WILL GET A REAL TIME SATELLITE ITINERARY REPORT TO SUBSTANTIATE THEIR FOOT PRINT EVEN IN AN ANOTHER TIME ZONE .

HOW TO MAKE LOSS IN BUSINESS

WHY EYE BELIEVE WALKING TOURISM IS NECESSARY FOR TOURISM BECAUSE OF REAL TIME AND IT WILL HELP TO SAVE THE HUMAN LIFE IN EARTH . IN THIS WORLD WHERE HUMAN FEET HAVE BEEN ANCTICIPATED BY TECHNOLOGY MEANS WHERE THE MOVEMENT OF PEOPLE IN ADVANCE AND IN FACT IT BECAME TRUE WITH THE REAL TIME AND THIS WHOLE EPISODE HAS BEEN SHOWCASE IN HISTORY . TO UNDERSTAND THIS THEORY OF ANTICIPATED FEET , NEED TO TO MORE CAUTIOUS . IN THIS MODERN ERA OF TECHNOLOGY WE ONLY ANTICIPATE A FEET WHERE IT MOVE TO BUT WE DON'T HAVE THE EXACT TIME OF THIS FUTURE MOVEMENT BUT WE FIGURED OUT THE ANTICIPATED FEET IN THE HISTORY LOCATION OF SATELLITE SPACE REPORT . THIS IS THE KIND OF CONCEPT WHERE AN ENTREPRENEUR CAN THINK ABOUT TO INVEST MORE INTEREST ON IT BECAUSE THIS CONCEPT IS FULLY RELATED TO ALL HUMAN BREATHING LIVES .

FREE IMAGE OF SPACE WALK

FREE IMAGE OF SPACE WALK IN SIDE EARTH

FEEE IMAGE OF GROUP TRAVEL WITH SPACE THROUGH SATELLITE REPORT

AS WE KNOW THE BIG THINGS WE SEEING ON EARTH LOOKS VERY SMALL AT ABOVE THOUSANDS FEET OF SEA LEVEL.CAN ANY ONE IMAGINE THE SIZE OF STARS WHO ARE DWELLING BILLIONS OF MILE UP ABOVE THE SKY AND EVEN WE DON'T KNOW MUCH MORE THE FACT OF THESE SMALL SPARKLE STARS. JUST IMAGINE WHEN A HUGE AIRBUS OR A HUGE BOEING AIRCRAFT LOOKS SO VERY SMALL AT 35.000 FEET UP ABOVE THE SKY LEVEL THEN EYE DON'T THINK ANY SCOPE WOULD HAVE BEEN AVAILABLE TO MEASURED UP SIZE OF ANY SINGLE STAR EXCEPT A HUGE DEVASTATION . THATS ONLY REASON TOURISM IS NECESSARY FOR BETTER UNDERSTANDING OF THING ,PLACES , PEOPLES. THE SALIENT FEATURES OF WALKING TOURISM LIES WITHIN HUMAN .AS AN ENTREPRENEUR IF EYE DEVELOP THIS WALKING TOURISM PRODUCTS THEN EYE CAN IMAGINE AN OFFICE OF HUGE PROFIT .

LETS END UP THIS 1ST CHPTER " HOW TO MAKE LOSS IN BUSINESS" WITH THIS TRAVEL AGENCY AND OUT BOUND TOUR OPERATION SET UP , TOURISM PRODUCTS DEVELOPMENT AND FEW TIP OF FINANCIAL ACCOUNT. IN NEXT CHAPTER WE WILL DISCUSS THE STEPS TO UNDERSTAND THE CONSUMER BEHAVIOUR AND MARKET RESEARCH FOR TRAVEL AND TOURISM , DISTRIBUTION MANAGEMENT OF DEVELOPED TOURISM PRODUCTS . INTERNATIONAL MARKETING TO CREATE IN BOUND TOURISM BUSINESS AND A PROJCTED LONG TERM FINANCIAL ANALYSIS AND TRADE PROFIT&LOSS AND PROJECTED BALANCE SHEET OF TOURISM TRAVEL OFFICE TO ENVISAGE A HUGE PROFIT.

HERE EYE MEANS I AND READERS CAN RELATE TO THEMSELVES WHILE READING THE BOOK .

AUTHOR OF "HOW TO MAKE LOSS IN BUSINESS' WITH MOTHER

DETAIL INFORMATION ABOUT THE BOOK :-
AUTHOR -: GYAN CHAND PATTANAYAK
COMMUNICATION NUMBER -:
+91 7681830729
+91 7853045594

9 798889 594857

Printed by Libri Plureos GmbH in Hamburg,
Germany